Diary of a Service Dog (Dropout)

Story by Kristen An Horton
Art by Heidi Anne Horton Pittman

Zea Books

Lincoln, Nebraska

Diary of A Service Dog (Dropout)
©Copyright 2019 Kristen An Horton
Illustrations ©Copyright 2019 Heidi Anne Horton Pittman

ISBN 978-1-60962-164-3

Zea Books are published by the University of Nebraska-Lincoln Libraries

Electronic (pdf) edition available online at
http://digitalcommons.unl.edu/zeabooks/

Print Edition Available from http://lulu.com/spotlight/unlib

Nebraska
UNIVERSITY OF
Lincoln

UNL does not discriminate based upon any protected status.
Please go to http://www.unl.edu/equity/notice-nondiscrimination

for H. Granger Shaw Horton, the most loyal and loving dog

Thank you Judy, Maddy, Anisha, and Liz: aka UNL TEACH 854

Thank you Vicki, Richie, Paul, Jared, and Granger's "Aunt" Roz

-Kristen

Dear Diary:

August 26
My name is Granger. I have finally been adopted! I'm so excited to meet my "furever" family. I'm going on an adventure!

September 1

I'm jealous of my new friend, Froggie. He's a frog and I am a Labrador Retriever – Golden Retriever mix. I want to swim around all day.

September 15
I have no idea what a chinchilla is, but I really want to chase this funny looking bundle of fur! Where did my new cat friends go? I like to play with them.

October 31

What kind of spooky zoo house did I move into? A pink-toed tarantula named Diggle is my eight-legged fuzzy friend. Her feet tickle when she sits on my head.

November 12

I thought I was a dragon slayer. Today I found out I am going to be a BALANCE ASSISTANT SERVICE DOG, but I have no clue what that means.

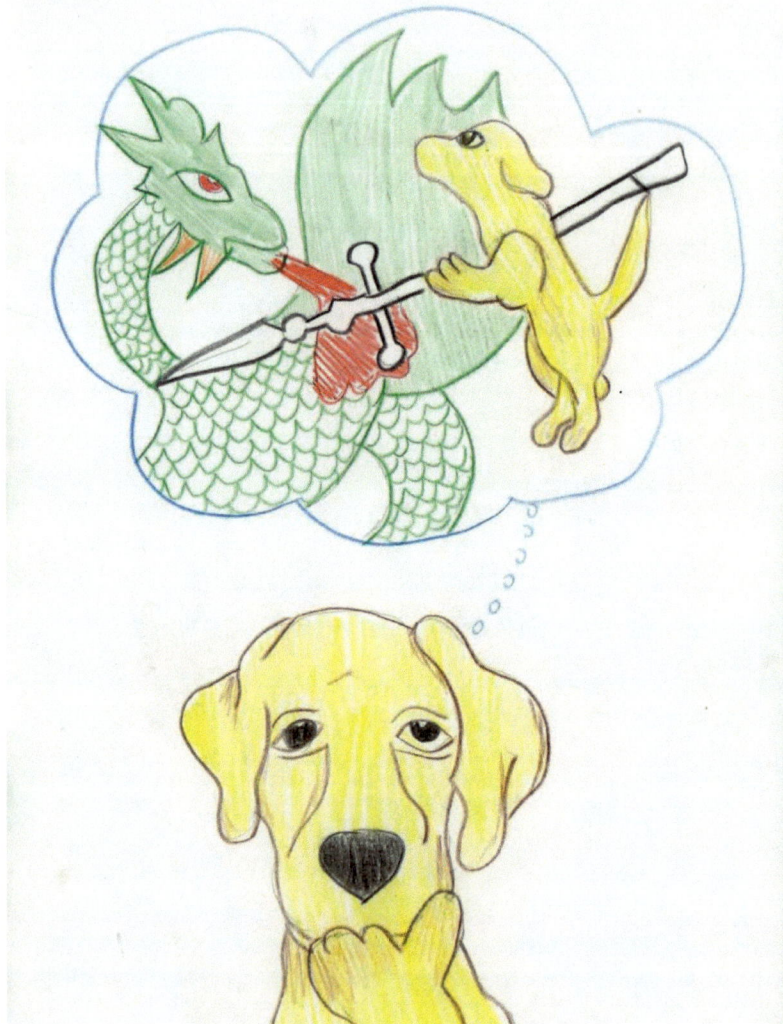

December 25

My new uniform lets people know that I am in training to be a service dog. I learned service dogs take care of their human. I already do that! I get to go everywhere with her which is way cooler than slaying dragons!!

January 2
This is "training"? All I am doing is playing and having so much fun!

January 19
There is no such thing as bad weather, just the wrong outfit!
How cute are my new snow boots!?!

February 5

I live in Lincoln, Nebraska. It's cold outside. I know I'm sleeping on the job. Don't judge me: I am still paying attention to my human.

February 29

I have mastered the skill of carrying stuffed animals all the way up the stairs while keeping an eye on my human.
[Note to self: When does training start?]

March 1

I spoke too soon. I have been training this entire time!
Learning to pick up things, carry them, and walk next to my
human are all part of being a good service dog.
Dig it, I'm really a service dog!

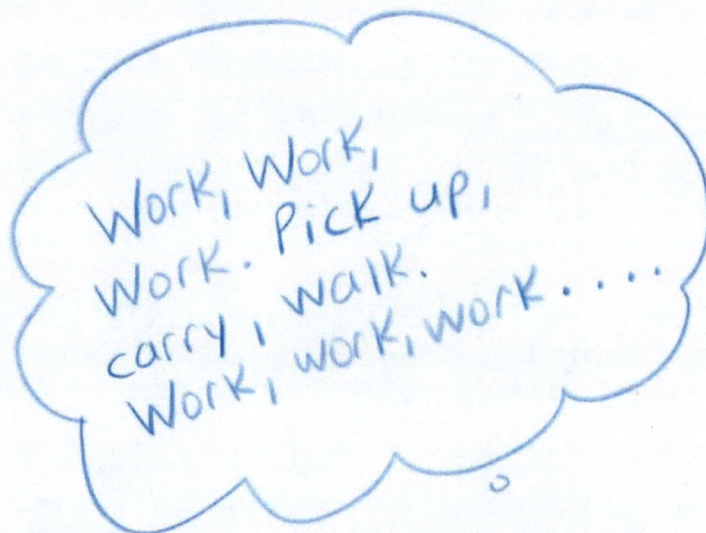

March 14

Training can be so exhausting. Focusing on my human and carrying a ball. I was tricked into training.

[Note to self: maybe I should go back to slaying dragons.]

April 2

Training lasts for hours, days, and months. Sit! Down! Up! Left! Right! Lights on! Lights off! Open door! Shut door! Pick it up! Walk backwards! Kitty, are you listening to me? Cats never think outside the box!

May 4

Seriously. Kitty, I'm trying to tell you how much time and hard work goes into becoming a BALANCE ASSISTANT SERVICE DOG. I know so many commands, while still focusing on my human. But I can't get distracted by any of the noises, people, and things all around me. You try doing that!

June 18
I passed a very hard test and now I'm a certified service dog!
Check out my new uniform! I'm cute. I know it. I'm working!
[Note to self: must remember when I'm wearing my uniform I
can only pay attention to my human.]

July 24

I'm flying!! The loud noise doesn't even bother me.
The flight attendant gave me a pair of wings for my uniform.
I know other dogs are so jealous of my *bling*.

August 10
Kitty! Get off of my new uniform!!!
No wonder I leave the house everyday covered in fur!

September 4

It's so hot outside! I'm talking into the fan and it's making my bark *quiver.*

[Note to self: don't get too close to the fan!!!]

October 31

It's been an entire year since I met my "furever" family! It feels like I've aged at least seven years. Guess what my Halloween costume is?

I'm a three-headed dog called a cerebus!

November 4
I rocked the vote! I cast my first ballot, and it was for a presidential election!
[Note to self: be there for my human.]

November 15

I'm an activist! I walked in a rally with lots of other service dogs and their humans. I met a guide dog for a human who can't see. Humans with disabilities have rights too! I'm very special — a BALANCE ASSISTANT SERVICE DOG.

[Note to self: Do not, under any circumstances, let my human fall down.]

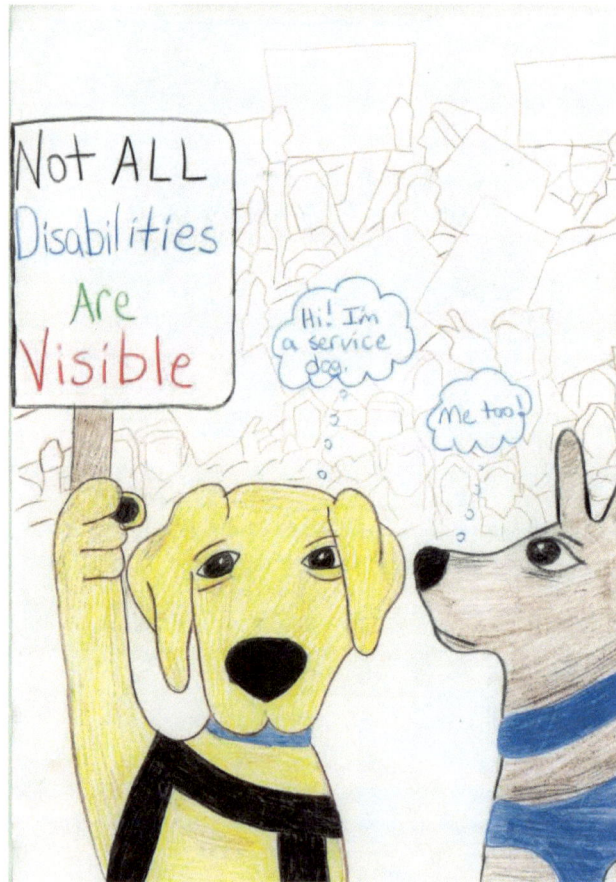

December 2

Oh no! I got scared today when a tiny human my height ran at me shrieking in excitement. I growled and barked.

Please remember that when you see a service dog, we are at work.

It's okay to ignore us!

December 15

No matter how many years of training I have, I am still a dog.
Now I growl and bark at every person, big and small, who
comes near my human. I want to protect her from everyone.
I'm so sad because I can't focus on my human.
[Note to self: I need to work on holding in my anger.]

January 4

I've been stripped of my royal title! I spent so much time and energy training, and my certification was gone in an instant. I have to stay home while my human leaves. I know there is something more important I should be doing.

[Note to self: What am I going to do if I'm not a service dog...?]

January 20
I know! Slay dragons!!

February 14
It's my entire fault! My human fell because I wasn't there to help her balance while she walks.
[Note to self: I let my human down. I failed.]

March 7
But my human still loves me, and I am still a good service dog
... at home!!

March 31

Wait! Am I all washed out? Am I doomed? Is there hope?

Goonies never say die!

I'm back in training! Let the new adventures begin!

"Service Dog Dropout" by Kristen An Horton

to the tune "Beauty School Dropout"
song by: Frankie Avalon
songwriters: Richard Finch and Harry Casey
©Sony/ATV Music Publishing LLC

Your journey sad to tell,
A shelter dog done well,
Most mixed up certified service dog on the block.
Your future's so unclear now,
What's left of your career now?
Can't even take a walk without a growl.
Service dog dropout,
No certification any more.
Service dog dropout,
Snarled at kids and barked at the door.
Well at least you spent all your time,
To play and tear your toys up.
After slaying all the dragons,
To have the human pick the stuffing up.
Doggy stop growling,
(Better stop growling)
Why do you give everyone such a fright?
Why are you barking?
(Why are you barking?)
You know the rules but don't act right.
If you go for a new certificate you would no longer feel ridicule.
Turn in your canine teeth and go back to training school!
Service dog dropout,
(Service dog dropout)
Barking at anyone you approach.
Service dog dropout,
(Service dog dropout)
It's time you were above reproach.

Well they've already taught you everything,
You know you're not a bully.
But no people want to go near you,
Unless you behave fully!
Doggy don't bite it.
(Don't bite it)
You're not cut out to be so mean.
Better just leave it,
(Leave it)
Who wants their dog to cause a scene?
Now your nails are trimmed,
Your fur is groomed,
But still the work is draining,
Put on your uniform and go back to training.
Doggy don't mess up,
Don't let your human hit the ground!
Doggy you shape up,
Your human still wants you around!
Now you know the chore,
Get off the floor,
You really gotta try,
Gotta be going back to training that's why.
Service dog dropout
(Service dog dropout)
Go back to training
Service dog dropout
(Service dog dropout)
Go back to training
Service dog dropout
(Service dog dropout)
Go back to training

Author's Note

Granger is the best service dog I could ever want. I got him when he was 10 months old. Even before we started training, he knew what I needed from him. I have Meniere's Disease and vestibular migraines. Essentially, I have vertigo all the time with non-stop tinnitus. I don't look like I need a service dog. My disability is invisible. I can pass as an able bodied person. Because of that, young teenagers harassed us on public transportation; one even pulled his tail. A toddler ran at us waving chopsticks in the air. No matter how well trained a dog is, he is still a dog. His instinct to protect me was overriding his thousands of dollars of training. When his trainer suggested I re-home him and get a new service dog, I said no way. Granger is my dog and I am his human. He is in remedial training.

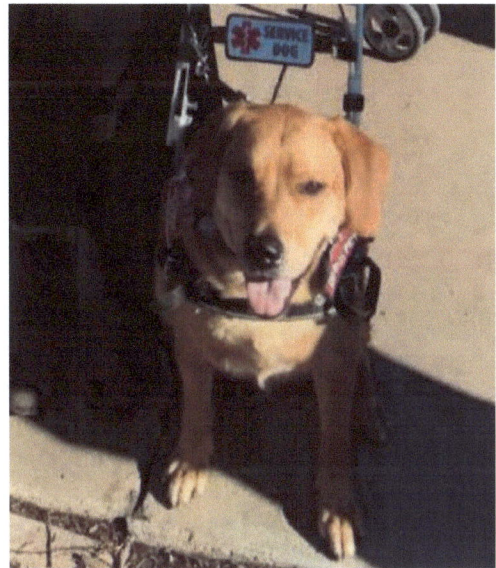

The most important take away is that the public, children and adults, need to learn how to not interact with service dogs. As Granger says, "I'm cute. I'm working. Please ignore me."

www.ingramcontent.com/pod-product-compliance
Lightning Source LLC
Chambersburg PA
CBHW042011080426
42734CB00002B/46